TRUE **LIGHT**

A, superior, take, unto, the, premier, haloing, of, tenuation.
Readily, available, True Light, provides, resource, into,
time's, motifed, and, vestuved, authenticate, revelation.

LARK VOORHIES

iUniverse, Inc.
New York   Bloomington

True Light
A, superior, take, unto, the, premier, haloing, of, tenuation.
Readily, available, True Light, provides, resource, into,
time's, motifed, and, vestuved, authenticate, revelation.

iUniverse books may be ordered through booksellers or by contacting:

iUniverse
1663 Liberty Drive
Bloomington, IN 47403
www.iuniverse.com
1-800-Authors (1-800-288-4677)

Because of the dynamic nature of the Internet, any Web addresses or
links contained in this book may have changed since publication and
may no longer be valid. The views expressed in this work are solely those
of the author and do not necessarily reflect the views of the publisher,
and the publisher hereby disclaims any responsibility for them.

ISBN: 978-1-4502-4354-4 (pbk)
ISBN: 978-1-4502-4355-1 (ebk)

Printed in the United States of America

iUniverse rev. date: 7/5/2010

THE LIGHT

For, ages, we, have learned, to, search, for, the, truth, about, life. The, truth, in, regard, to, the, opolous, insight. Facts, ascertaned, according, to, the, willing, advance, of, theme, and, time. Fames, tolled, apart, from, steads. Standards, partrolled, in, union, with, the, ever, held, age, perfection, within, the, stales, of, solution. New, boaders, of, parental, discovery, taled, to, the, wind, of, true, shelter, and, distine. At, harmony's length, we, trivail, the, chiefs, of, known, ability, to, prevail, the, pronounce, of, hartmanship.

By, the, tides, we, have, carry, to, the, answer, and, rotation, of ,the, prime, station, of, known, proof. That, the, composite, effective, has, windtried, the, focal, placement, of, real, treasure. The, earnest, complace, knows, for, suit, the, esponsible, inloadings, trust, upon, the, tried, and, true.

Among, the, known, born, contemporaries, it, is, this, light, this, ircandantinal, life, that, brings, us, to, harvest's, center. From, the, antythipical, awaining, to the, prodigiginous, call, life, and, its, luminant, theory, has, banted, profile, unto, prologue, for, hypurbiant, best. True, to, Zenith, mile, performance, for, and, to, the, greatance, quote, of, destiny, would, have, renile, aprose, close, warning.

Apraisal, honn the, elect, of, stroke, keys, aplanthremary,

unto, the, strength, of, prose, of, inroad, wherein, the, correct, plithany, in, regard, to, atroph, may, be, all, ahieght, unto, the, pure, passings, of, windtales, and, ritters.

Path, aflight. There, is, no, new, trail, whererin, to, remean, the, particification, upon, the, now, exposed, cues, of, entrance, and, colomn. The, winthrical, overmeans, of, partismanship, and, jantor. The, whole wron, enlightenment, upon, title, to, the, markread, and, the, plightened.

About, the, ages, there, have, nestered, the, monuments, of great title, discriminant hope, and, surmounting belief. Filaments, of, awailed, value, to, which, the, expand, of, intrigue, and, conscience, can, be, accredited. There, awaitened, through, to, the, status, achieve, are, the, precipitals, enlightened, to, the, conscious, aware. Staples, of, harness, and, virtue, decorate, the, enthrall, amidst, the, symposing, swall, of, huened, sentiment. Sincere, prite, of, motive, appears, gesturate, to, the, indibted, scene. Bold, proasts, align, the, tall, order, for, archive, and, verse. Stalls, of, geneer, wrail, the, plentitude, emobssened, apros, the, prepository, effective, about, the, very, still, of, theory, and, apreive.

Now, at, cross, are, the, bearing, root, of, handsomely, tied, followings, gained, to, the, instill, of, reap. Sheatherened, callows, of, date, and, morost, that, so, charge, the, all, too, probable, appliqué, awenst, the, carolous, sweep, aprost, the, known, terrain, of, harmonous, journalings.

New, to, the, aprailing, substantiation, of, entidinal, call, happen, the, joustlings, of, apravious, conjeer. True, to, plate, the, inscribable, incastings, peer, remove, from, the, incrational, and, or, formal, entries. Apar, attune, the, instile, approximate, ziquester, we, aim, along, the, tannicle, reach, to, forment, baldestine, presentry.

Polite, to, creation's, arrest, go, the, reflective, response, of, the, ever, bountiful, production, combined, attuned, the, most, thought, and, foreseen, replentures, are, the, ever, cast, prologues, protaled, unto, the, all, amystic, grodentures.

Pleasantly, apprapo, to, the, arrangement, there, alogged, you, find, areas, of, great, truth, and, cultivate, candor. Don, to, most, are, the, reposit, realties, that, indeed, induce, gain, upon, the, clearical, mount, there, thus, aprained.

Due, atide, are, the, lone, nest, pridngs, at, view, apros, the, windtrical, teil, at, modum. The, guise, at, prost, deals, a, wornthrical, blow, amight, the, adued, newcast, of, prite, afortined, the, lowell, of, enthrall, fornightal, to, Winhelsinger's, reparted, title. Thereby, and, therefore, we, arrive, amidst, the, pordentinal, outplaste, awhole, by, martens, guilests, and, bordentures. Coined, aside, and, aturned, unto, there, are, reels, of, beguise, unpared, and, without, compare, tonned, on, const, replenst, replast, and, resense. Dauted, rains, substate, moust, divide, post, the, trane. Till, we, prot. Then, we, trait. We, have, light.

Created by: Lark Voorhie

LIGHT

- **Genesis1:1-5** - In the beginning God created the heavens and the earth. Now the earth proved to be formless and waste and there was darkness upon the watery deep; and God's active force was moving to and fro over the surface of the waters. And God proceeded to say: "Let light come to be." Then there came to be light. After that God saw that the light was good, and brought about a division between the light and the darkness. And God began calling the light Day, but the darkness he called Night. And there came to be evening and there came to be morning, a first day.

There are many beginnings in the bible. In this beginning, as you see here, the earth, later known as the lands, the nations, or, the, world, begins within a, formless, darkness, later known as the expanse. In, biblical, language, it is of import, to agree upon the authenticity, of its celestial, authorship, being that, the divine illustrator, himself, is noted to have authored, much, if not all of its inscribings, through the active hand of human standings. Always, it is, noteworthy, to have, on hand, the natural, emphasis, of phrase, upon which, one, can, build, ,an, organic, relation, to, the, surrounding, forces, that, be.

Now, as the force was active, moving to, and, fro, depositing, and, energizing, all that was needed for, existence, and, life, it, can be, asserted, God, himself, remained busy, in the, demonstration, and, design, of, the, prevailing, and, off prime, nebula. Once , the, combination, was, satisfactory, He, the, Divine, One, Himself, could, then, convene, the, famous, antithipus, most associated with, creation, itself, "Let there be light." And, well, the rest, is history.

- Genesis 8:22 - For all the days the earth continues, seed sewing and harvest, and cold and heat, and summer and winter, and day and night, will never cease.

Join, me, in this grand quest, of origin. As, we, explore, the, scape, of, supreme, arcomferency, toward, scale, and, task, and, plight. This, is, the, book, of, heraldings. This, is, the, book, of, sight. This, is, the, all, explanatory, form, upon, destiny. This, is, the, book, of, light.

As, we, uncover, the, lengths, widths, Heights, and, depths, of, antithical, mystery, aboard these, vested, intratures, take, heart, for the swell, of, life. Reservations, are, few, aside, this, innermost, quelling, of, travel. And, the, fantastic, ever, cheers, the, ageless, quasiatic, tender. If, science, can, explain, our, origin, yet, cannot, duplicate, it, from, where, do, we, unearth, its, finesse, of trapping? If, the, order, we, tangle, with, what, is truly, limitless, by, design, To what source, do, we, accredit, the, educational enwrapping? None, can, explain, the, earth, so, exquisitely, as the, early, pioneers. Those, ripefull, and, witness, to, our, coveted, ingenter.

From, the, cannons, recovered, of, long, ago, one, can, delineate, formula, for, and, or, of, the genius, of, creation. How, to, capture, maintain, and, form, it, into realenture.

Throughout, this, ledger, you, are, indeed, invited, to, takes, note, of, some, of, the, earliest, recordings, of, original, destiny. Its advance. Its renown. Its intrail. Par, example:

- **Psalms 97:11** - Light itself has flashed up for the righteous one, and rejoicing even for the ones upright in heart.

Now, the flashing of the light, institutes, a, transposed, mode, of thought. As, God, is introduced, as having thick gloom. Then, lightenings flash, all, around, him. Announcing righteousness, and, judgment, in consumption of his adversaries, all, around. As, the earth saw, and, came to be, in, severe, pains. What, does this mean? It's, a, pronouncement. Of, divine, proportions. Carrying, those, who, err. Warning, those, who, by, conscience, bear, the, gravity, of, not, falling, short.

It, is, a universal, hailing. A, grand, court, case. Calling, all, opposing, gods, into, account. This, centrific, scope. This, advent, for, the, light, is, a, theme, that, can, be, traced, to, the, earliest, most, well, known, writings.

There, is, a, theme, in Psalms, similar, in, scale, as, it, depicts, and, defines, thread, to, light. This, great, rush, of, the, masses, to, commune, bondage, to, times, before, knowing. The, many, ways, to, touch-down, into, origin. We'll, begin, with, the, pursuit, for, light. Truth, as, it, is, sacredly, defined. For, it, is, the, most, sought after, indelible.

- **Esther 8:16** - For the Jews there occurred light and rejoicing and exultation and honor.

Here, the, light, is, used, to, markate, celebration. As, victory, over, foreign, territory, had, been, gained, and, won. Queen,

Esther, in, radiant, symbol, of, that, light, shown, prudence, and, appreciation, to, be, the purse, of, vigilant, splendor.

- **Job 22:28** - And you will decide on something and it will stand for you; And upon your ways light will certainly shine.

Here, it is, spoken, of Job, as, triumphing, over, his three, contenders. God, having, pronounced, him, innocent, in, one, of, the, highest, judicial, decisions, since, the, disastrous, rebellious, bumfumblery, atwixt, the, Garden, of, Eden. Here, Job, had, lost, everything. Family, wealth, land. All, to, come to meeting, with, an, array, of, false, comforting, hoarders, of, the, spirit. Amidst, the, ailing, Job's predicament, he, to, God, makes, plea. Upon, council, and, examination, he (God), sees, fit, to, bestow, upon, Job, the, complete, and, immediate, reuttance, of every, and, all, contribaned, attachment. Thus, the, above, award, of, the, light.

In, the, bible, light, depicts, and, plays, an, interesting, character . There, are, modes, of, protect, modes, of, defense, and, fight. Modes, of, interial, intrigue, carving, path, to, inhales, of, insight. Whether, heroic, or, antagonistic, visceral, or, downplayed, light, portrays, an, integral, part, into, the, portion, through, which, we, exist. Dare, not, deny. We, need it. For, it, is, a, crucial, inlay, in, recommend, of, the, very, fabric, that, would, be, our, future, and, life.

It, is, known, for, every, award, granted, there, has, been, reward, earned. Yet, how, does, one, earn, light? If, we, explore, the, realm, of, it, one, comes, to, find, the, effective, modes, through, which, light, is, not, only, contracted, but, received, in, define. Let's, take, a, closer, look, into, light. Its, origin. The quest, for, glory, and, its, measures, of, inceit.

One, entrail, in, particular, is, the, psalms, from , the, biblical, cannon. Let's, peer in, to, its, codex, of, luminescent, treasure.

- **Psalms 112:4** - He has flashed up as a light in the darkness to the upright ones. He is gracious and merciful and righteous.
- Isaiah 58::10 - And you will grant to the hungry one your own soulful desire, and you will satisfy his soul that is being afflicted, your light also will certainly flash up that is in the darkness, and your gloom will be like midday.
- Psalms 37:6 - And, he will certainly bring forth righteousness, as, the, light, itself, and your justice as at the midday.
- Micah 7:9 - The raging, of Jehovah I shall bear - for I have sinned against him - until, he conducts my legal case and actually conducts justice for me. He will bring me forth to the light; I shall look upon his righteousness.
- Malachi 3:18 - And you people (through light) will again certainly see the distinction between a righteous and a wicked on, between on who is serving God and one who has not served him.
- Matthew 7:2 - For with what judgment you are judging, you will be judged; and with the measure you are measuring out, the will measure out to you (again, through light).
- Isaiah 58:8 - "In that case your light will break forth just like the dawn; and speedily would recuperation, spring up for you. And before you your righteousness would certainly walk; the very glory of Jehovah would be your rear guard."
- Proverbs 4:18 - But the path of the righteous ones is

like the light that is getting brighter and brighter until the day it is firmly established.

Psalms, speaks, in, abbreviate, outline, the, jonst, for, taking, steps, to, the, light. Having, thanksgiving, its, primal theme. And, the, taking, in, of, wisdom, and, knowledge, apassed, amongst, household, and, farvor, its, very, mean. Further, it, notes: "The wicked one is plotting against the righteous one." However, "Better is the little of the righteous one, than the abundance of the wicked ones." So, then, it, would, be , the, doing, of, good, and, the, turning, away, from, bad, that, grants, the, light, in, this, case. What, is, more, "The mouth of the righteous is the one that utters wisdom in an undertone...The law of his God is in his heart" "Hope in Jehovah and keep his way." Apparently, here, it, is, the, earth, that, is, garnished, as, the, receive. It, scores, on, in regard, to, a, "waiting, attitude." Now, in, relation, to, overturning, wicked, deeds, with, good, ones, there, is, this, timely, element. Interestingly, enough, passage, relays, the, sending, of, messengers, in, translation, of, these, age, old, inspired, gifts. Don't, however, fail, to, remember, the, grander, theme: the, celestial, court, case. The, trial, of all, antiquity. It, in, fact, is, above, the, case, of, the, light, for, this, timeline, and, ours, in, import, of, the, guarantee, of, our, very, survival. Full, of, parable, there, are, many, distinctions, drawn. Specifically, in, chapter, 7, of, Matthew. Where, we, have, the, highlight, of, that, narrow, gate. In, finale, we, discover, underscored: "Yet day after day it was I (God) whom they were seeking, and, it was in the knowledge of my ways that they would express, delight."

Now, that, we, outlined, stream, of what we, aspire, let us, delve, still, deeper, into, the, comprised, history, of, "Whom", When", and, "Why".

- **1 Peter 2:9** - But you are "a chosen race, a royal

priesthood, a holy nation, a people for special possession, that you should declare abroad the excellencies of the one who called you out of darkness into his wonderful light.

Here, a, distinction, does, indeed, take, place. Here, the, itemization, and, compartment, of, those, who, are, and, those, who, are, not, is, indeed, standing. Here, full, of, example, the, second, book, of, 1st Peter, is, indeed, in, lead, as, to, the, known, interiors, in, regard, to, how, a, thing, is, earned. A, deeper, look, would, show, us, "why", the, above, scripture, has, relevance, to, us, in, this, time. Let, us, proceed:

- **Isaiah 51:4** - "Pay attention to me, O my people; and you national group of mine, to me give ear. For from me a law itself will go forth, an my judicial decision I shall cause to repose even as a light on to the peoples.
- Psalms 119:105 - Your word, is a lamp to my foot, and a light to my roadway.

In, this, genealogy, plays, an, important, role. Here, The, Israelites, are, being, buffed, in, preparation, of, receipt, of, their, inheritance, upon, repentance, and, recovery, of, law. They, are, made, promise, upon, guarantee, of, abidance, to, the, provision, of, indelible, script Scrolls, of, prophecy, in, descript, of, manner, operation, and, level, of, coincide. Here, Psalms, in, parthenium, heralds, the, way.

In, Samuel, the, very, initialization, of, divine, royalty, instruction, is, laid, to, blueprint, task, on, par. Let's, share, a, closer, look.

- **1 Samuel 2:9** - The feet of his loyal ones he guards; As for the wicked ones they are silenced in darkness, for not by power does a man prove superior.

- Psalms 37:28 - For Jehovah is a lover of justice, and he will not leave his loyal ones. To time indefinite they will certainly be guarded; But as for the offspring of the wicked ones, they will indeed be cut off.
- Zephaniah 1:15 - That day is a day of fury, a day of distress and of anguish, a day of storm and of desolation, a day of darkness and of gloominess, a day of clouds and thick gloom.

Here, we, delve, into, sewery. Appropriate, esteem, in, remittance, to, appropriate, measures. There, are, countless, entries, within, the, extreme, of, these, cannons. Yet, none, like, the, ever-ensuing, battle, of, good, against, evil. From, these, installments, we, gain, insection, into, the, heat, of, the, gate. The, heart, of, choice, right, at, the, gheln. Here, we, have, the, two-sides, to, loyalty, and, their, finish. As, well, as, scrutinous, wisdom-based, instruction, for, the, future, heavenly king. Involved, are, the, very, notes, to, destiny. Keying, in, we, guard, with, finality, the, thoroughness, in, relation, to, response. The, balance, of, span, makes, for, a, keen, text, of, interest. Who, are, truly, righteous? Where, lie, the, wicked? What, indeed, is, evil?

A, brief, scoping, upon, the, above, said, mentioned, queries, a, thought-provoking, in-depth, rich, in, appointment. We, begin, with, the, narrative, of, the, woman, Hannah. Mother, to, the, prophet, Samuel. She, indulges, a, refined, commentary, on, the, faith, of, an, inherent, people. On, the, one, hand, we, have, those, rightly, disposed, for, honor, and, glory, and, height. On, the, other, there, are, the, ones, who, carry, on, in, disrespect. The, Psalms, are, rich, within, quarter, of, this, distinction. And, in, Zephaniah, we, find, correlation, to, the, pre-flood, conditions, in, Genesis. Where, "God, felt, regret, that, he, had, made, man, at, all."

Nevertheless, there, is, extended, invitation, to, survive. Gaining, light, and, adhering, to, exacting, devotion. It, states: "And I will give attention to those…filling the house of their masters with violence and deception…the men…who are saying in their heart, 'Jehovah will not do good, and he will not do bad.'" It, also, relates, to, say, "Jehovah is a killer and a preserver of life, a bringer down into She'ol and he brings up. Jehovah is an impoverisher and an enricher, an abaser also an exalter."

So, you, see, if, the, deeds, of, the, wicked, are, in, fact, to, be, considered, evil, and, are, to, be, cut, off. And, the, commitment, to, legality, would, indeed, define, what, is, right, which, is, to, be, rewarded. Then, the, end, suits, the, means, is, as, suffice, to, say, as, it, is, wise, not, to, be, mislead, because, one, reaps, what, one, sews.

Now, then, how, do, we, really, acquire, light? Further, along, we, will, discover, the, formula, and, method, required, to, advance, in, possession, of, this, highly, prized, find.

- **Proverbs 6:23** - For the commandment is a lamp, and a light the law is, and the reproofs of discipline are the way of life.
- Proverbs 4:13 - Take hold on discipline; do not let it go. Safeguard it, for it itself is your life.
- Hebrews 12:11 - True, no discipline seems for the present to be joyous, but grievous,; yet afterward, to those who have been trained by it it yields peaceable fruit, namely, righteousness.
- 2 Peter 1:19 - Consequently we have the prophetic word made more sure; and you are doing well in paying attention to it as to a lamp shining in a dark place, until day dawns and a daystar rises in your hearts.
- Deuteronomy 18:15 - A prophet from your own midst,

from your brothers, like me, is what Jehovah will raise
up for you - to him you people should listen.

Within, Proverbs, there, lies, the, greatest, esotricity, for, the,
containment, of, light. In, book 6, of, the, Proverbs, there,
intale, the, complete, antithesis, to, the, hazard-laden, road.
"Observe, O my son, the commandment of your father, and
do not forsake the law of your mother. Tie them upon your
heart constantly; bind them upon your throat. When you walk
about, it will lead you; when you lie down it will stand guard
over you; and when you have waked up, it itself will make you
its concern. In, book 4, the, timeline, is, set to advise, one's,
adherence, to, healthier, measures, in, mode. "My son, to, my,
words do pay attention. To my sayings incline your ear. May
they not get away from your eyes. Keep them in the midst of
your heart. For they are life to those finding them and health
to all their flesh. More than all else that is to be safeguarded,
safeguard your heart, for out of it are the sources of life."

From, Hebrews, we, have, closing, statement, to, the, halls,
of, light. Reminders, of, order, and, the, setting aright, all,
afooted, paths. Now, the, breadth, of, this, book, contains,
some, of, the, most, concentrated, advice, of, any, and, all,
cannons, in, relation, hereto. Gems, of, wonder, and, esteem,
align, the, ways, of, wonder, and, esteem, to, encourage, one's
boister throughout, the, pavings, of, discipline. To, take, shape,
rather, than, being, destroyed, by, the, dallings, of , the, rod.
Tender, in, portrayal, yet, firm, in, approach, Hebrews, delivers,
enthralling, render, of, the, champion, of light.

In, Peter, it, speaks, of, the, need, for, escape. This, is,
intriguing, on, account, of, two, reasons; for, it, wells, the,
question: From, what, are, we, in, vanture, against? And: Just,
how, do, we, make, it, through, to, arrive? Now, this, brings,
into, question, the, purpose, of, prophecy. Its, origination.

Its, meaning. Its, all-in-all, value. The, truth, of, its, status, amongst, those, deprived, of, understanding. Where, shall, we, begin? Let, us, start, by, scoring, the, elementary, formula, for, aligning, one's, self, to, reception. In, the, first, chapter, we, find: "Forasmuch as his divine power has given us freely all things that concern life and godly devotion, through the accurate knowledge of the one who called us through glory and virtue…in all earnest effort, supply to your faith virtue, to your virtue knowledge, to your knowledge self-control, to your self-control, endurance, to your endurance godly devotion, to your godly devotion brotherly affection, to your brotherly affection love." It, furthers, in, reasoning, in, guarantee, of, desired, outcome. Promising, hope, upon, remittance. Whatever, the, care, such, cannonity, can, hardly, be, considered, beneath, worthy, of, the, investment, it, engenders.

Now, let's, revel, a, bit, earlier, into, the, original, manuscript, for, such, guising.. In, Deuteronomy, we, encounter, blueprint, to, divine, authorship, to, authority, itself. Here, the, creator, staples, injuct, onto, mainframe, of, physical, law. Highlighting, interview, with, protrigal, formats, atwist, themes, and, amuses, refined. Upon, scope, and, view, we, can, sense, the, official, meters, outlaid, within, such, a, challenge. Those, faultless, and, blessed. Those, guilt, and, found, in, detest.

Yet, how, is, the, telling, of, such, monument, truly, to, be, conceived? How, in, light, of, authentic, tracings, does, this, purest, of, instruct, hone, through, to, real, attaintance? These, amongst, further, theories, adjuncts, survival, of, the, light, we, shall, indeed, rapture. For, he, quotes: "A prophet I shall raise up for them…and I shall indeed put my words in his mouth, and he will certainly speak to them all I shall command him."

- **Malachi 4:5** - "Look! I am sending to you people

Eli'jah the prophet before the coming of the great and fear-inspiring day of Jehovah.

- Joel 2:31 - The sun itself will be turned into darkness, and the moon into blood, before the coming great and illustrious day of Jehovah arrives. (Old Testament - A.D.)
- Acts 2:20 - The sun will be turned into darkness and the moon into blood before the great and illustrious day of Jehovah arrives. (New Testament - B.C.)
- 2 Peter 3:10 - Yet, Jehovah's day will come as a thief, in which the heavens will pass away with a hissing noise, but the elements being intensely hot will be dissolved, and earth and the works in it will be discovered.

Here, we, can, connote, the, import, of, visceral, comprehension. Also, the, the, object, of, what, one, would, want, to, escape. Take, in, mind, the, third, book, of, the, second, letter, form, Peter, for, it, states: "For, according, to, their, wish, this, fact escapes, their, notice, that there were a heavens of old and an earth standing compactly out of water and in the midst of water by the word of God; and by those means the world of that time suffered destruction when it was deluged by water. But by the same word the heaven and the earth that are now stored up for fire and are being reserved for judgment and of destruction of the ungodly men." So, you, see, presently, in, our, day, therein, lies, the, need, to, survive, the, coming, fires, of, this, world. How, does, one, measure, up, for, qualifications, that, survive, this, tested, fire? Be, it, literal, or, symbolic, one, would, quest, institution, amongst, choice, wisings, in, order, to, indell, specifications, upon, this, dubital. Let, us, define, further.

- **Psalms 101:3** - I will not set in front of my eyes any good-for-nothing thing. The doing of those who fall away I have hated; It does not cling to me.

- Romans 15:4 - For the things that were written aforetime were written for our instruction, that through our endurance and through the comfort of the scriptures we might have hope.
- 1 Peter 1:10 - Concerning this very salvation a diligent inquiry and careful search were made by the prophets who prophesied about the undeserved kindness meant for you.
- 2 Timothy 3:16 - All scripture is inspired of God and beneficial for teaching, for reproving, for setting things strait, for disciplining in righteousness.

Psalms 101, is, telling, in, the, ways, one, must, exhibit, in, order, to, quality, this, income. Beginning, with, verse, three, it, provides, the, clearest, advise, on, how, to, mold, one's, self, a, recipient, of, this, light. It, speaks, further, about, discretion. About, gaining, the, power, over, faultless, qualities, in, order, to, achieve, optimum, reception. Describing, the, outcome, early, on.

The, cannon, speaks, on, about, responsibility, toward, those, upon, whom, lay, claim, to, this, descript, upon, lucent, chronology. Labeling, them , akin, to, starquest, features. For, the, purpose, that: "Namely these, nations, might, prove, to, be, acceptable, it being sanctified.

The, first, book, within, the, first, letter, from, Peter, speaks, of, inheritance. It, describes, them, as, incorruptible, and, unfading. It, also, speaks, of, a, last, period, of, time, through, which, prophesies, would, foretell, avenues, one, may, begin, to, look, to, seek, and, find, its, source. In, promotion, of, the, effort, required, it, insights, a, preem, of, instructional, in, highlight, of, the, rush, of, activity. It, embraces, the, order, to, do, with, along, with, that, which, can, be, done, without. In, lead, it, adverts, the, rewarded, rules, of, conduct. Describing, its, value, marking: "But, the, saying, of, Jehovah, endures, forever."

In, the, third, book, within in, the, second, letter, to, Timothy, we, are, served, warning. And, are, steered, clear, the, decomposition, of, behavioral, trappings, that, would, find, one, disapproved, therefore, preventing accumulate. "From, these, turn, away". Provided, there, is, encourage, in, the, end. "And yet out of it all the lord delivered. Me."

By, examining, prophecy, more, closely, you, learn, endowment, of, code. Defend, of, find. And, security, upon, gain. Below, are, in, depth, reviews, in, regard, to, prophesy, its, origin, and, the, future, of, its, divide.

- **2 Peter 1:21** - For prophecy was at no time brought by man's will, but men spoke from God as they were born along by holy spirit.

Now, we, understand, foreknowledge, to, be, of, import, stipened, and, record. Yet, who, are, the, involved? Of, what relevance, are, they, concerning, us? The, edificiate, inherent, deserves, satisfying, debriefing, as, its, indelible, inner workings, are, equally, stationed, on, trial.

Here, prophecy, is, spoken, of, as, "accurate, knowledge." That, we, by, comportmentality, applying, thereby, gain, access, into, formula, of, appraise. For, it, states: "Through these things he has freely given us the precious and very grand promise, that through these you may become sharers in divine nature, having escaped the corruption that is in the world through lust." - 2 Peter 1:3,4 It, is, unfailingly, by, way, of, this, course, that, one, can, arrive, in-line, the, awarded, prize. Truth, being, the, epitome, in, markation, it, further, intrails, for, those, such, desiring, to, "become eyewitnesses, of, his, magnificence." - 2 Peter 1:16

Yet, how, is, this, done? Through, read, alone? Let, us, take, up, context, to, these, well, guarded, thoroughly, tucked, transcripts, to, really, unearth, source, and, brandishment.

- **Job 29:3** - When he caused his lamp to shine upon my head, when I would walk through darkness, by his light.
- Psalms 18:28 - For you yourself will light my lamp, O Jehovah; My God himself will make my darkness shine.
- Ephesians 5:13 - Now all the things that are being reproved are being made manifest by the light, For everything that is being made manifest is light.

The, great, mappings, alabyrinthed, in, recharge, of, biblical, cannon, lead, us, here, to, Job. One, of, the, greatest, installments, of, predate, and, prerecord. The, 29th, book, indeed, depicts, a, man, of, glory, and, wealth, of, station. Having, lost, all. Themeing, his, quest, of, return. In, light, of, the, all, age, pursuit, one, must, care, to, guard, and, lead, by, paths, of, vested, succeed. Within, this, abbreviate, hold, immeasurable, standard, to, triumph. Enumerations, of, staple. The, aggregate, upon, initiate, paragon.

Now, no, road, to, victory, is, without, astay. No, worthy, ascendancy, avex, the, tone, remarked. That, proclaimed, one, should, expect, indeed, the, precocity. Fine, out, adwelst, the, scribing, again, of, Psalm (book 18), we, mett, out, solutionary, institute. Here, David, the, King, of, Jerusalem, takes, length, in, note, despite, the, impending, despoils, to, petition, clear, route, unto traverse, of, gain. Stating: "He, was, rescuing, me, because, he, had, found, delight, in, me." And, further:

"A shield he is to all those taking refuge in him…And who is a rock except our God? The true God is the one girding me closely with vital energy, and he will grant my way to be perfect."

In, Ephesians (book 5), there, lies, yet, still, law, for, the, succeeding. Along, with, ample, warning, repellant, of, block, and, stumble. Wherefore,: "Awake, O sleeper, and arise from the dead." Individual, beware.

LIGHT

In, reference, to, Isaiah, and, Esther, here, again, there, is, spoken, of, as, light, a, woman. Here, in, symbol, she, takes, station, acorporate, the, most, profound, prophecy, taking, part, within, canonical, history. The, edifice, upon, which, all, engaging, prophecy, was, construct. Within, Genesis, there, remain, the, elements, that, theme, out, to, fulfill, all, 66, cannons, of, this, book, of, prophecy. Take, a, look, below.

- **Genesis 3:13-15** - With that Jehovah God said to the woman: "What is this you have done?" To this the woman replied: "The serpent - it deceived me and so I ate." And Jehovah God proceeded to say to the serpent: "Because you have done this thing you are the cursed one out of all the domestic animals and out of all the wild beasts of the field. Upon your belly you will go and dust is what you will eat all the days of your life. And I shall put enmity between you and the woman and between your seed and her seed. He will bruise you in the head and you will bruise him in the heel."

Here, inlies, the, drama. After, Adam, and, Eve, had, without, the, proper, permission, taken, of, the, fruit, of, the, tree, of, the, knowledge, of, good, and, bad, they, had, just, fallen, short, and, and, therefore, rebellious, to, God's, miscible, law, of, request, and, thanksgiving. Apart, from, becoming, history's, first, sinners, they, now, had, obligate, to, recompense. Thus, the, above, prophecy. If, indeed, sin, intailed, death, its, end, there, was, then, needed, adequate, contract, to, see, forth, surviving, generates. For, God, had, then, stated, "Here, the, man, has, become, like, one, of, us, in, knowing, good, and, bad, and, now, in, order, that, he, may, not, put, his, hand, out, and, actually, take, fruit, also, from the tree of life and eat and live on to time indefinite -" With, that, god, put, them, out. And, us, with them. So, you, see, this, gabe, to, survive, has, steeper, meaning, involved, I'm sure, than, you, intended, upon, before, the, reading, of, this, book. Eye, opening, legalities, that, demand, render, through, to, account.

- **Isaiah 60:1** - "Arise, O woman, shed forth your light, for your light has come and upon you the very glory of Jehovah has shone forth.

Here, we, have, again, this, "woman." T'is, not, Eve, for, she, had, sinned, and, lied, to, god, boldfaced, in, regard, to, her, crime. This, woman, is, now, symbolic. God's, jewel. For, he, says, "I myself, the Lord, have called you in righteousness, And I proceeded to take hold of your hand. And I shall safeguard you and give you as a covenant of the people, as a light of the nations, for you to open the blind eyes, to bring forth out of the dungeon the prisoner, out of the house of detention those sitting in darkness." This, authority, to, conjure, such, feats, of, action, or, not, free, or, in, separate, from, responsible, incount. Lighting, further, is, states, "Likewise let your light shine before men, that he may see your works and give glory to your father who is in the heavens." Now, this, elemental, invise, is, only, as, rich, as, you, keep. Save, injuring, replicates, to, teenial, transpires. For, it, sharpens: "That you may become blameless and innocent, children of God without a blemish in amongst a crooked and twisted generation, among whom you are shining as illuminators in the world."

Living, in, agreement, of, survive, how, does, one, operate, in, discrete? And, indeed, how, does, one, know, there, is, mode, of, receipt, of, light? In, a, shifting, climate, in, what, lou, doe, one, authenticate, true, light? Reading, on, T'is, simple, degrate. For, it, tales: "He will go before him with Elijah's spirit and power, to turn back the hearts of fathers to children and the disobedient ones to the ones to the practical wisdom of righteous ones."

Further, it, inclines: "For you the sun will no more prove to be a light by day, and for brightness the moon itself will no more give you light. And God must become an indefinitely lasting light, and your beauty." "And to you who are in fear of my name the sun of righteousness will certainly shine forth, with healing in its wings; and you will actually go forth." So, this, light, would, indeed, not, body, from, the, material. "A light for removing the veil of the nations." This, indeed, would, become, God's, instituant. "Also, night will be no more, and they have no need of lamplight nor do the have sunlight, because God the Lord will shed light upon them, and they will rule as kings forever and ever."

Therefore, if, we, were, to, harness, the, invest, one, would, denote, greater, accument, aboust, the, self-incur, reinmobent, upon, not, only, the, therial, quesensts, abroad, loinquotious, vestings, but, also, the, primeheathal, endowings, character, of, archetypal, enjests. Therefore, How, does, does, the, light, behave? How, do, you, at, all, recognize, it, at, quality, and, value? As, we, continue, foremoth, these, and, further, matters, shall, indeed, become, catoptric. Read, further, and, you, shall, see.

- **Isaiah 51:17** - "Rouse yourself, rouse yourself, rise up, O Jerusalem, you who have drunk of the cup of Jehovah's rage. The goblet, the cup causing reeling, you have drunk, you have drained out."
- Isaiah 52:1 - Wake up, wake up, put on you strength, O Zion! Put on your beautiful garments, O Jerusalem, the holy city! For no more will there come into you the uncircumcised and the unclean one.
- Isaiah 58:1 - "Call out full-throated: Do not hold back. Raise your voice just like a horn, and tell my people their revolt, and the house of Jacob their sins."

In, contrast, we, find, here, in, Isaiah, denunciation, for, intent, on, living, in, opposition, to, the, light. Which, is, why, he, structs, further, "Listen to me, you people who are pursuing after righteousness, you who are seeking to find the lord." "Pay attention to me, O my people; and you national group of mine, to give me ear. From me a law will go forth, and my judicial decision I shall cause to repose even as a light to the peoples." Now, here, there, is, clear, warning, of, the, opposing, choice. Indeed, one, is, in, must, to, braile, the, outscope, of, apocalyptic, inmeasures. For, he, sets, here: "Listen to me, you the ones knowing righteousness, the people in whose heart is my law."

So, this, we, surmise, is, a, legal, recoupenment. The, Divine One, himself, has, taken, a, position, of, mercy, in, regard, to, those, blind, and, unable, to, decipher, accurate, law. He, calls, out, with, the, strength, of, holy, arm. Even, entitling, himself, a, "mighty, man, of, war." With, complete, intent, upon, the, gather, of, those, who, would, respond, the, pro, war, call. Shielding, avaluate, intention, amongst, bleethened, morall. Thus, he, charges, the, finality: "He will likewise startle many nations. At him kings will shut their mouth, because what had not been recounted to them they will actually see, and what they had not heard they must turn their consideration."

In, conclusion, here, I, recommend, the, full, book, of, Isaiah, in, that, no, where, else, can, there, be, found, "Listen to me, you the ones powerful at heart, you the ones far away from righteousness...Bring you controversial case forward," says Jehovah. "Produce your arguments, " says the king of Jacob. "Produce and tell to us the things that are going to happen. The first things - what they were - do tell, that we may apply to our heart and know the future of them. Or cause us to hear even the things that are coming. Tell the things that are to come afterward, that we may know you are gods. Yes, you ought to do good or bad, that we may gaze about and see it at the same time. Look! You are something nonexistent, and your achievement is nothing. A detestable thing is anyone that chooses you...I am Jehovah. That is my name; and to no one else shall I give my own glory." There, is, further, "I, Jehovah, the First One; and with the last ones I am the same." Also, "'Come, now, you people, and let us set matters strait between us,' says Jehovah. 'Though the sins of you people should prove to be as scarlet, they will be made white just like snow; though they should be red like crimson cloth, they will become even like wool...But if you people refuse and are actually rebellious, with a sword you will be eaten up; for the very mouth of Jehovah has spoken it.'" So, you, see, we, can, find, encouragement, in, the, true, fact, that, "Nations will certainly go to your light, and kings to the brightness of your shining forth."

Amen.

- Isaiah 49:6 - And he proceeded to say: "It has been more than a trivial matter for you to become my servant to raise up the tribes of Jacob and bring back even the safeguarded ones of Israel; I also have given you for a light of the nations, that my salvation may come to be to the extremity of the earth."

- Luke 2:32 - A light for removing the veil from the nations and a glory of your people Israel.

The, extremity, of, the, earth, this, light, was, to, reach. How, is, that so? Psalms 19:6 - "From one extremity of the heavens it is going forth, and its finished circuit is the other extremities; And there is nothing concealed from its heat." He is making wars to cease to the extremity of the earth." Mark 13:27 - "And then he will send forth the angels and will gather his chosen ones together from the four winds, from earth's extremity to heaven's extremity." Acts 131:47 - "'I have appointed you as a light of nations, for you to be a salvation, to the extremity of the earth." Genesis 1:3 - "And God brought about a division between the light and the darkness."

Division: T'is, important, to note, once, having, come, to, a, complete, and, final, accuracy, inpon, resource, the, obligate, to, option, operate. For, He, states, again, in, verse, 18, "To make a division between the light and the darkness." And, in, verse, 4, "God saw that the light was good."

We, can, now, define, light, to, be, many, things. Let, us, go, in-depth, gaining, indicate, as, to, its, elemental, composite, its, muli-deflne, of, role, and, its trazure, of source.

- **Isaiah 9:2** - The people that were walking in the darkness have seen a great light. As for those dwelling in the land of deep shadow, light itself has shone upon them.
- Matthew 4:16 - The people sitting in darkness saw

a great light, and as for those sitting in the region of deathly shadow light rose upon them.

Here, of, more, concern, is, the, end. All, twixed, the, beginning. Thus, ahailed: "Again, I, am, writing you a new commandment, a fact that is true in his case and in yours, because the darkness is passing away and the true light is already shining." Wherefore, "God is light and there is no darkness ay all in union with him." Thus, of, major, import, is 1 Kings 18:21, where, it, asks, the, question: "How long will you be limping upon two, different, opinions?

Now, if, indeed, option, is, to, pray, on, what, basis, do, you, cant, choice? Mantle, this, "The one alone having immortality, who dwells in unapproachable light, whom not one of man has see or can see. To him be honor and might everlasting. Amen." -1 Timothy 6:16

- Matthew 5:16 -Likewise let your light shine before men, that they may see your fine works and give glory to your father who is in the heavens.

Here, we, have, reason, to, be, at, peace. In, Matthew, book, 5, inlays, a, step-by-step, sure, guide, to, a, oneness, with, the, light. Here, for, example, it, is, quoted, "Happy are those conscious of their spiritual need." Let, us, take, a, moment, to, consider, this. The, many, forms, through, which, the, spirit, is, in, contrast, and, in, compatibility, to, the, light. Romans 7:23, explains: "But I behold another law of my members warring against the law of my mind and leading me captive to sin's law that is in my members." With this opposition, there, lies, composite, delineation, in, render, of, triumphed, subject, to, pro vs. con. Galatians 5:16, clears, this, up, for, us, quite, nicely. As, it, states, "But I say, keep walking by spirit and you will carry out no fleshly desire at all." Now, where, the, flesh, equates, sin, we, need, further, clarification, to, remain, adequately, paved. It, speaks, on, in, outline, of, the, fruitage, of, the, flesh, then, goes, on, to, itemize, the, surviving, elements, that, make, for, a, fool, proof, endowment, of, spirit. Proving, untainted, blameless. A, functional, vital , composition, that, no, succeeding, voyager, of, this, life, should, do , without.

- Ephesians 5:8 - For you were once darkness, but you are now light in connection with the lord. Go on walking as children of light.
- John 12:36 - While you have the light, go m walking in the light, in order to become sons of light.

LIGHT

- **John 3:19** - Now this is the basis for judgment, that the light has come into the world, but men have loved the darkness rather than the light, for their works were wicked.

" Most truly I say to you, unless anyone is born again, he cannot see the kingdom of God." "For he that practices vile things hates the light and does not come to the light, in order that his works may not be reproved. But he that does what is true comes to the light, in order that his works may be manifest as having been worked in harmony with God." "He that does not receive reproof, will die."

So, here, we, have, an, out take, of, a, very, general, theme, to , the, standard, of, life. Those, who, wish, to, advance, play, by, the, rules. "For he does not give the spirit by measure." Thus, book 3 of John, holds, in, its, stead, theme, to, purification. Its, benefit. Its, formula. Its, inherit, gender. We, can, render, further, in, regard, the, definisis, of, this, precious, resource. Its, conception. Its, rise. Its, achieved, end.

- **John 1:9** - The true light that gives light to every sort of man was about to come into the world.
- John 9:39 - "For this judgment I came into the world: that those not seeing might see and those seeing might become blind."
- John 12:47 - "I came not to judge the world, but to save."
- John 3:16 - "For God loved the world so much that he gave his only-begotten son, in order that everyone exercising faith in him might not be destroyed but have everlasting life."

Now, if, at the end, of the light, is, the, pot, of, gold, referred, to, as, everlasting, life, what exactly, is, the, ratio, of, demand, to, resource? Also, if this, ventured, pursuit, holds, key, to, the, lifeblood, of, your, very, exist. How, vital, it, is, then, to met, out, the, quality, of, its, remaining, availability. 1 Corinthians 7:29 - "The time left is reduced." Galatians 4:10 - "You are scrupulously observing days and seasons and months and years." Genesis 49:1 - "Gather yourselves together that I may tell you what will happen to you in the final part of the days." For, he states: "It has become the final part of the time in which to know me."

- **Luke 4:18** - "Jehovah's spirit is upon me, because he anointed me to declare the good news to the poor, he sent me to preach release of the captives and sight to the blind, to send the crushed ones away with a release.
- John 12:46 - "I have come as a light into the world, in order that everyone putting faith in me may not remain in the darkness."
- John 9:5 - "As long as I am in the world, I am the world's light."
- John 8:12 - "I am the light of the world, he that follows

me will by no means walk in darkness, but will possess the light of life."

Now, here, the, annals, are, pressing, for, comprehension, regarding, the, light, of, life. Its, freeing, properties. Its, crud, rarity. Its, ored, commodity.

- **John 1:5** - And the light is shining in the darkness, but the darkness has not overpowered it.
- John 12:35 - "The light will be among you a little while linger. Walk while you have the light, so that the darkness does not overpower you; and he that walks in the darkness does not know where he is going."

As, the, sun, sets, and, we, are, upon, the, dusk, of, knowledge, it, is, wise, to, coarse, ones, granted, position. In, the, mainstay, of, exist, this, is, a, must. The, race, is, on. Contenders, muster, up.

- **Job 24:13** - As for them, they proved to be among the rebels against the light; They did not recognize its ways, and they did not dwell in its roadways.
- Isaiah 5:20 - "Woe to those who are saying that good is bad and bad is good, those who are putting darkness for light and light for darkness, those who are putting bitter for sweet and sweet for bitter."

With, no, confusion, as, to, your, sides, you, may, know, proceed, goal, aim, and, objective. With, objectives, equipped, you, may, now, headway, the, betterment, of, statum.

- **John 12:48** - "He that disregards me and does not receive my sayings has one to judge him. The word that I have spoken is what will judge him in the last day."
- Deuteronomy 18:19 - "And it must occur that the man

who will not listen to my words that he will speak in my name, I (God) shall myself require an account form him."

- Ephesians 4:22-24 - That you should put away the old personality which conforms to your former course of conduct and which is being corrupted according to his deceptive desires; but you should be made new in the force actuating your mind, and should put on the new personality which was created according to God's will in true righteousness and loyalty.

LIGHT

Now, that, we, have, briefed, the, coordinates, of, light, knowledge, understanding. Let, us, realm, still, more, in-depth, the, premit, in, connection, to, projection, upon, stages, of, wealth, therein.

- **2 Corinthians 11:14** - Now what I am doing I will still do that I may cut off the pretext from those who are wanting a pretext for being found equal to us in the office of which they boast. For such men are false apostles, deceitful workers, transforming themselves into apostles of Christ. And no wonder for Satan keeps transforming himself into an angel of light.

False, light? Possible? Yes. As, the, above, text, preimphantly, highlights, there, exists, a, stage, of, lucient, no, greater, in, value, than, fool's, gold. Let, us, investigate, this, property, quality, derivity.

- Galatians 1:8 - However, even if we or an angel out of heaven were to declare to you as good news something beyond what we declared to you as good news, let him be accursed.

- Luke 2:10 - "Have no fear (an angel), for, look! I am declaring to you good news of a great joy that all the people will have."
- Genesis 12:3 - "And I will bless those who bless you, and him that calls down evil upon you I shall curse, and all the families of the ground will certainly bless themselves by means of you."
- Zechariah 8:23 - "This is what Jehovah of armies has said, ' It will be in that day that ten men out of all the languages of the nations will take hold, yes they will actually take hold of the skirt of a man who is a Jew, saying: "We will go with you people for we have heard that God is with you people."
- Luke 1:73 - The oath that he swore to Abraham our forefather.

So, much, is, at, steak, that, conditions, are, set, as, to, who, will, receive, and, at, what, level. Some, as, heirs, some, as, prophets; the, list, goes, on. Proof, is, in, the, recording: "You are the sons of the prophets and of the covenant which God covenanted with your forefathers, saying to Abraham, ' and in your seed the families of the earth will be blessed.'" - Acts 3:25

- Galatians 3:8 - Now the scripture, seeing in advance that God would declare people of the nations righteous due to faith, declared the good news beforehand to Abraham, namely: "By means of you all the nations will be blessed."

Again, the, round, id, genealogy vs. inheritance vs. qualification. Within, these tiers, we, conclude, and, secure, placement, among, the, first, finders. The, record, being: "Happy is the man to whose account Jehovah does not put error, and in whose spirit there is no deceit...I shall make you have insight and instruct you in the way you should go. I will give advice with my eye upon you." - Psalms 32:2,8 "To it all nations must stream." - Isaiah 2:2 "He will certainly render judgment among the nations and set matters strait respecting many peoples." - Isaiah 2:4 "The great day of Jehovah is near. It is near, and there is a hurrying of it very much...Neither their silver or their gold will be able to deliver them in the day of Jehovah's fury; but by the fire of his zeal the whole earth will be devoured. - Zephaniah2:14,18 "Therefore keep yourselves in expectation of me...till the day...for my judicial decision is to gather nations, for me to collect together kingdoms, in order to pour upon them my denunciation, all my burning anger; for by the fire of my zeal all the earth will be devoured." - Zephaniah 3:8 "All the nations of the earth will bless themselves due to the fact that you have listened to my voice." - Genesis 22:18

- Acts 13:48 - When those nations heard this, they began to rejoice and to glorify the word of Jehovah and all those rightly disposed for everlasting life became believers.

Here, we, take, note, and, or, are, witness, to, the, scramble, for, life. The seats are placed. Foreordination, is, set. Time, and, application, the, ticket. How, are, we, to, appeal, for, audience, amongst, the, survivors? The, below, entries, embrace, timeless, aphorisms, keen, to, the, conversion, of, thought, to, status.

- Romans 1:16 - For I am not ashamed of the good news; it is, in fact, God's power for salvation to everyone having faith.
- Mark 8:38 - For whoever becomes ashamed of me and my words in the adulterous and sinful generation, the Son of man will also be ashamed of him."
- Matthew 12:30 - "He who is not for me is against me, and he who does not gather with me scatters."

- 1 Corinthians 2:16 - For "who has come to know the mind of Jehovah, that he may instruct him?"

Here, it, is, of, key, note, to, attend, the, import, of, what, is, being, spoken. With, time, on, the, march, and, position, in, high, demand, one, would, do, well, to, identify, and, settle, the, establish, subsidiary, to, grant.. Ahead, are, selective, leafs, of, adage, to, consider. For, he, thinks, this, way. "And he is of one mind, and who can resist him?" - Job 23:13 Followed, by, the, timely, addition, to, "Be of the same mind in the Lord." - Philippians 4:2 "Quit being fashioned after this system of things, but be transformed by making your mind over, that you may prove to yourselves the good and acceptable will of God." - Romans 12:2. For, "The god of this system has blinded the minds of the unbelievers, that the illumination…might not shine through." - 2 Corinthians 4:4 Therefore, "Keep your minds fixed on the things above, not on the things upon the earth." - Colossians 3:2 How? "I will put my laws in their mind, and in their hearts I shall write them. - Hebrews 8:10 Therefore, "Brace up your minds for activity, keep your senses completely; set your hope…that is to be brought to you at the revelation." - 1 Peter 1:13. Yes, by, affixing, ourselves to the above, standard, one, is, able, to, aver, sight, to, the, supreme, affirmation, and, thereby, proclaim, title, amongst, the, elite, few.

LIGHT

Here, we, open, acquaintance, to, the, proprietor, of, the, illustrious, objective, himself. Politely, we, engage, upon, rapture, into, such, celebrated, introduction. The, pilgrimage, wholly, enlightening. The, jaunt, an, education, to, proper, voyage. The, peregrination, one, of, fame, eminence, veneration, and, odyssey. Now, the, wizard, may, unveil. For, only, he, knows, the, rites, and, formats, on, veil, to, thus, produce, the, aturned, mode, of, relativation. Let, us, stay, a, moment, to, renown, our, host, of, sight. Shall, we?

- 1 Timothy 6:16 - The one alone having immortality, who dwells in unapproachable light, whom not one of men has seen or can see.

Here, we, encounter, upon, the, amazing, phenomena, of, God, Himself. Dwelling, alone, within, his, unapproachable, light. Save, the, moments, of, crucial, and, necessary, bursts, of, enlightenment. As, in , the, case, of, Paul (Acts 9:3), who, was, stopped, reproved, and, insighted, against, evildoing, on, the, part, of, his, being, called, to, the, path, of, light (Acts 22:6). Or, as, with, John (1:16), called, into, revelation, by, way, of, the, light, of, his, chief, ambassador. Now, as, with, their, works, then, forward (1Peter 3:18), that, onlooker, in, observance, of, their, example, might, be, led, to, God (Matthew 25:37-40), might, come, to, know, understanding, in, regard, to, the, light (John 14:19). All, be, it, known, let, it, be, stated, to, clear, that, not, all, who, have, sight, see, and, not, all, who, have, light, really, live. The, following, chapter, will, cover, this, quite, succinctly. However, now, we, must, in, record, keep, this, in, mind:

- James 1:17 - "Every good gift and every perfect present is from above, for it comes down from the Father of the celestial lights, and with him there is not a variation of the turning of the shadow.

Amen.

LIGHT

While, we're, here, let, us, journey, back, to, the, origin. Our, genesis. From, Revelation, through, to, the, first, cannon. Let us, voyage, this, destined, passage, of, world, and, place. Thought provoking, and, relinquishing, in, transposal, to, imminent, chronicle. In, abbreviate, this, is, the, history, of, light.

- Revelation 21:14 - "Nations will walk by means of… light, and the kings of the earth will bring their glory into it."
- 1 John 1:7 - "If we are walking in the light as he himself is in the light, we do have a sharing."
- 1 John 1:5 - "And this is the message which we have heard from him and are announcing to you, that God is light and there is no darkness at all in union with him."
- 1 Thessalonians 5:5 - For you are all sons of light and sons of day. We belong neither to night nor to darkness."
- Ephesians 5:13 - "For everything that is being made manifest is light."

- Ephesians 5:9 - "For the fruitage of the light consists of every sort, of goodness and righteousness and truth."
- Ephesians 5:8 - "For you were once darkness, but you are now light."
- 2 Corinthians 6:14 - "Do not become unevenly yoked with unbelievers. For what fellowship do righteousness and lawlessness have? Or what sharing does the light have with darkness."
- 2 Corinthians 4:6 - For God is he who said: "Let the light shine out of darkness, " and he has shone on our hearts to illuminate them with the glorious knowledge of God."
- 1 Corinthians 4:5 - Hence do not judge anything before the due time…the Lord…will both bring the secret things of darkness to light and make the counsels of the heart manifest, and then each one will have his praise come to him form God."
- Romans 13:12 - "'The night is well along; the day has drawn near. Let us therefore put off the works belonging to darkness and let us put on the weapons of light."
- Romans 2:19 - "And you are persuaded that you are a guide of the blind, a light for those in darkness."
- Acts 22:6 - "Out of heaven a great light flashed."
- Acts 13:47 - "In fact, Jehovah has laid this commandment upon us in these words, 'I have appointed you as a light of nations, for you to be a salvation to the extremity of the earth."
- Psalms 148:3 - "All you stars of light."
- Psalms 138:11 - "Then night would be light about me."
- Psalms 119:130 - The very disclosure of your word gives light."
- Psalms 119:105 - "Your word is a lamp to my foot, and a light to my roadway."

- Psalms 118:27 - "Jehovah is the Divine One, and he gives us light."
- Psalms 112:4 - "He has flashed up in the darkness as a light…He is gracious and merciful and righteous."
- Psalms 104:1,2 - "Bless Jehovah, O my soul…Jehovah my God, you have proved very great. With dignity and splendor you have clothed yourself, enwrapping yourself with light as with a garment.
- Psalms 89:25 - "Happy are the people…O Jehovah, in the light of your face they keep walking."
- Psalms 76:4 - "You are enveloped with light, more majestic than the mountains of prey."
- Psalms 43:3 - "Send out your light and your truth. May these themselves lead me. May they bring me to your holy mountain and your grand tabernacle."
- Psalms 36:9 - "For with you is the source of light; by light from you we can see light."
- Psalms 18:28 - "For you yourself will light my lamp, O Jehovah; my God himself will make my darkness shine."
- Psalms 4:6 - "Lift up the light of your face."
- Genesis 1:18 - "To make a distinction between the darkness and the light."
- Genesis 1:5 - "God began calling the light Day, but the darkness he called Night."
- Genesis 1:4 - "And God saw that the light was good."
- Genesis 1:3 - And God proceeded to say: "Let light come to be."
- Genesis 1:1 - "In the beginning God created the heavens and the earth."

LIGHT

"The getting of wisdom is O how much better than gold! And the getting of understanding is to be chosen more than silver." - Proverbs 16:16

We've, come, this, far. Let, us, now, plunge, the, ultimate, depth, into, the, defining, of, light, its, wisdom, the, understanding, and, life. Being, that, God, is, light, and, there, is, no, association, with, him, as, regards, darkness, how, exquisite, then, the, telling, of, its, advance, its, harness, unique, its, kieling, depth. Why, one, would, have, stayed, the, blind, not, to, sight, the, finishing, import, to, the, sheer, utter, wisdom, of, the, emanation, of, God's, keen, incline. Won't, we, now, seek, explore, the, truth, amidst, the, story, of, light.

Being, that, light, is, in, opposition, to, darkness, and, it, can, be, taken, from, the, original, forms, of, Greek, and, Hebrew, to, mean, or, refer, to, that, which, manifests, form, from, a, light-giving, body. We, can, thus, deduce, ultimately, God, to, be, the, supreme, proprietor, in, supply, of, this, vital, resousrse.

T'is, generally, followed, that, light, is, the, energy, source, carrying, within, it, wave, of, transmit. Qualities, in, combination, of, color, that, when, tanslated, over, the, limitless, acculmination, delight, the, eye, of, man. So, then, "Where, now, is, the, way, by, which, the, light, distributes, itself?" - Job 38:24

The, source, and, former, of, the, light, had, earlier, created, the, heavens. That, along, with, the, great, luminations: the, sun, the, moon, and, the, stars. All, by the relativity, of, his, word, "Let light come to be." Compare: Genesis 1:1-3, and, Psalms 136:7 -9.

Scriptural, cannons, repeatedly, associate, the, light, with its creator. Countless, entries, testify, in, rightness, to, this, regard. "Jehovah is my light and my salvation. Of whom shall I be in fear? Jehovah is the stronghold of my life. Of whom shall I be in dread?" - Psalms 27:1 Of, great, intrigue, is, that, there, exists, darkness, but, God, himself, has, no, toke, nor, identity, nor, connection, with. In, as, much, to, say, "And I saw, even I, that there exists more advantage for wisdom than for folly, just as there is more advantage for the light than for darkness." - Ecclesiates 2:13

Why, for, ageless, counts, he, has, first, been, hailed, as, the, epitomed, height, of, all, example, and, wisdom. Equating, light. "Give ear, O heavens, and, let me speak; And let the earth hear the sayings of my mouth. My instruction will drip as the rain, my sayings will trickle as the dew, as gentle rains, upon the grass." - Deuteronomy 32:1,2 Now, in, belief vs. truth, we, have, a wonderful, advantage, of, proof, in, regard, the, greatest, recordings, of, light. One, passage, in, mind, has, to, say, "For the comandment is a lamp, and a light the law is, and the reproofs of disclpline are the way of life." - Proverbs 6:23 For, "The Rock, perfect in his activity, for all his ways are justice. A God of faithfulness, with whom there is no injustice.

Righteous and upright is he." - Deuteronomy 32:4 "And they have no rest day and night as they say: "Holy, holy, holy is Jehovah God, the Almighty, who was and who is and who is coming." - Revelation 4:8

Yes, having, no, connection, in, the, fore, of, darkness, our, creator, and, all, who, carry, follow, and, or, abide, by, the, light, are, thus, unencumbered, by, the, common, and, degrading, practices, ultimately linked with darkness. Compare: Job 24:14-16, and, 1 Theselonians 5:7,8. Also: Ephesians 2:3, Romans 9:22, and, Romans 3:5 For, Jehovah, is, the, "father of the celestial lights." The, giver, of, the, sun, moon, and, stars. Preiminently, he, is, host, to, all, spiritual, enlightenment. The, source, of, all, known. "Pay attention to me, O my people; and you national group of mine, to me give ear. For, from me a law itself will go forth, and my judicial decision I shall cause to repose even as a light to the peoples." - Isaiah 51:4 For God is he who said: "Let the light shine out of darkness, and he has shone on our hearts to illuminate them with the glorious knowledge of God." - 2 Corinthians 4:6 Therefore, "By light from you we can see light." - Psalms 27:1

You, see, when , a, person, is, subject, to, the sight, of, wicked, thoughts, and, or, deeds, his perception, is, impure, and, he, is, susceptible, to, evil, design. He, is, in, great, spiritual, darkness. Compare:Matthew 6:23 Deutronomy 15:9, states, to, "Watch out for yourself for fear a base word should come into your heart." And, "They have eyes full of adultery and unable to desist from sin, and they entice unsteady souls. They have a heart trained in covetousness." can, be, sighted, by, 2 Peter 2:14. Therefore, by, way, of, detection, and, early, warning, we, are, able, to, identify, means, by, which, we, might, utilize, the, incorporate, of, prevention, as, these, signs, arise, and, are, addressed.

The "fruitage of the light" (Galatians 5:22), in, whole, exposes, the, baseness, of, the shameful, works, belonging, to, darkness. Compare: Ephesians 5: 3-18 Also:1 Theselonians 5:4-9 As, Romans 13:13,14 highlights, "As in in the daytime let us walk decently, not in revelries and drunken bouts, not in illicit, intercourse and loose conduct, not in strife and jealousy...do not be planning ahead for the desires of the flesh." Therefore, compare: Ephesians 6:11-18

With, all, constancy, apreen, the, favor, of, the, functional, format. Implore, the, cast, input, of, the, prosperous, way. Akeen, sensibility, to, honor, your, moral, strategem. At, paradigm, invest, wise. Shield, the, golden, precept. Choice, the, endeavored, plight.

Truly, intelligence, objectively, is, the, major factor, for, wisdom. The motivate, in, proper, planning, to, one's life course. The, book, of, Proverbs, is outstanding, in, fitting, adage. Boasting, of, station's affluency, it, safely, directs, one, to, the, thought well, of, God. Moreover, with, faith, being the assured expectation, of the things hoped, for. The, evident, demonstration, of, realities, though, not, beheld, one, requires, a higher, beakon, than, the, conventional, themes, one, is, accustomed, to, upon, elevate. - Hebrews 11:1 Fortunately, we, posses, at, our, aid, true, historical, recordings, upon, which, to, reference, for, sheer, position.

One, thought, in, mind; the, nuling's, power, to, communicate, transmission, unto, coveted, presup, carries, within, its, hallings, the, immote, force, to, grant, mount, to, the, prevailing, hattened, joust, by, way, of, thorough, kimberling. What, is, meant, is, this: if one, wisely, chooses, to, close, in, on, the, origin, why, not, choose, the, mapping, of, greatest, authenticity. The, earliest, cannon, in, conventional, known, is, the, bible. All, 66, books, co-written, by, the, the, one, hand, of, lovers, trustworthy, and, beloved, by, the, light. With, such, care, over, the, centuries, granted, who, could, doubt, the, framal, intention? "Moreover, without faith it is impossible to please him well, for, he, that, approaches, God, must believe that he is and, that he becomes the rewarder of those earnestly seeking him." - Hebrews 11:6 "For…all things are out of God." - 1 Corinthians 11:12

LIGHT

Being, that knowledge, is, acquainted, with, fact, Divine Wisdom, would be the ultimate, referral, to, use, of, fact. "O the depth of God, riches and wisdom and knowledge! How unreachable his judgments are and past tracing out his ways are! For 'who has come to know Jehovah's mind, or who has become his counselor?' Or, 'who has first given to him that it must be repaid to him?' Because from him and by him and for him are all things. To him be the glory forever. Amen." Compare: Romans 16:27 Also: Revelation 7:12 This, being, so, the, wisdom, personified, does, quote: "Buy truth itself and do not sell it." - Proverbs 23:23 For, it, professes, "Keep your eye on those who cause divisions and occasions for stumbling contrary to the teaching that you have learned and avoid them. For men of that sort are slaves, not of our Lord...but of their own bellies; and by smooth talk and complimentary speech, they seduce the hearts of guileless ones." Moreover, it, fosters, "Be wise to what is good, but innocent to what is evil." - Romans 16:17-19 Compare: The 23rd book of Proverbs.

Good, advice, for, God's, power is invincible. His, will, certain, of, success. His, ability, sure. "For all the gods of the peoples are valueless gods; But as for Jehovah, he has made the very heavens." - Psalms 96:5 "There is none like you among the gods, O Jehovah, neither are there any works like yours." - Psalms 86:8 Also: 1 Corinthians 8:6 Relentlessly, it, is, sighted, "You are my witnesses…in order that you may know and have faith in me, and that you may understand that I am the same One. Before me there was no God formed, and after me there continued to be none. I - I am Jehovah, and besides me there is no savior." - Isaiah 43:10, 11

Without, question, he, is, Sovereign, Lord, Supreme. The, Benevolent, Benefactor. Our, Creator. Without, his, having, made, the, physical, laws, cycles, and, standards, upon which, men, criterion, would, leave, nothing, in remain, on, which, to, build. A, simple, babble, of, confuse, and, compassed, theory, would, abide. Compare: Proverbs 3:19 Also: Jeremiah 10:21, 13 Instead, we, find, the God, of, moral, standing, to, proclaim, "For this is what Jehovah has said, the Creator of the heavens, He the true God, the Former of the earth and the Maker of it, He the One who firmly established it, who did not create it simply for nothing, who, formed it even to be inhabited: ' I am Jehovah and there is no one else'" Isaiah 45:18 "For God is a God not of disorder but of peace." - 1 Corinthians 14:33 "I am Jehovah; I have not changed." - Malachi 3:6 "SEE with what large letters I have written you." - Galatians 6:11

He, speaks further in axiom, stating, "Happy is the man listening to me by keeping awake at my doors…by watching at the posts of my entrances. For the one finding me will certainly find life." - Proverbs 8:35, 35

Of, greater, import, in, view, of, the, stately, physical, laws, which, garner, proof, of, our, ever, powerful, provenance, of, truth, and, power, are, the, moral, stationeries, vital, to, man's health, and, ultimate, well, being. Assured, there is nothing beyond, his, understanding. The things, spoken, by him, will, take, course, to, have, certain, success. Compare: Isaiah 55:8, 9 Also: Proverbs 9:10

LIGHT

"Do, not, become young children in powers of understanding…
be babes as to badness; yet become full grown in powers of
understanding." - 1 Corinthians 14:20

How, exactly, is, this, done? Book, 14, of, the, first, of,
Corinthians, is, rich, in, detail, the, settings, upon, which,
one, may, find, venue, amidst, the, endtrail, of, sought. Here, it
connotes: "Pursue love, yet keep zealously seeking the spiritual
gifts." And, further, too, "Let all things take place decently and
by arrangement."

This, abiding, to, become, understanding, can, be, well,
taken up within, the, biblical, cannon, of the book of Titus.
Here, we, press, on, to, advancing, knowledge. Where, it, is,
recorded: "For this reason…" you are to gain, in, powers, of,
understanding, that you might correct the things that were
defective…holding firmly to the faithful word…that he may be
able both to exhort by the teaching which is healthful, and to
reprove those who contradict. For there are many unruly men,
profitless talkers, and deceivers of the mind….This witness is
true…that the word of God may not be spoken of abusively.
These things are fine and beneficial to men." - Titus 1:5, 9, 10,

13, Titus 2:5, and, 3:8 Further, it, agrees, "That, after being declared righteous...we might become heirs according to a hope of everlasting life...upon the basis...which God, who cannot lie, promised before times long lasting." - Titus 3:7, and, 1:2

Titus 2:7, 8, indetails, the, lengths, to which, one, must assail, to, gain, the, acquired, vision, required, to, avail, light. Its, translation. Its, own, lasting, benefit. Verses, 12, 13, and, 15, continue, in, this, manner, abriefing, one, the, set, forth, to, triumphant, arrival, at, one's, quest, of, cycle.

In, essence, life, begets, life. Being, that, Jehovah, is, the, living, God, having, neither, a, beginning, nor, an, ending, life, has, always, existed, through, and, because, of, him. Jeremiah 10:10, expresses, "Jehovah is in truth God. He the living God and the king to time indefinite. Because of his indignation the earth will rock, and no nations will hold up under his denunciation." And, Daniel 6:26, cues, in, "Form before me there has been put through an order that, in every dominion of my kingdom, people are to be...fearing the God of Daniel. For he is the living God and the One enduring to times, indefinite, and his kingdom is one that will not be brought to ruin, and his dominion is forever." The, time, for, riposte, is, now. The, season, for, recovery, is, fast, approaching. The, guard, for, light, has, meted, out, stanchion, for, claim. Galatians 4:10, provisions, clue, instating, "You are scrupulously observing days and months and seasons and years." "Seek righteousness, seek meekness. Probably you may be concealed in the day of Jehovah's anger." - Zephaniah 2:3

In, addition, though, daily, substenance, is, met, more, is, required. For, man, must, also, satisfy, his, spiritual, measure. For, "It is written, 'Man must live, not on bread alone, but on every utterance coming forth through Jehovah's mouth.'" Matthew

4:4 (New Testimate) Deuteronomy 8:3 (Old Testimate) Yes, consequently, apart, from, man's spiritual provisions, there can , be, no, indefinite, continuance, of, life. Thus, recorded, is, profoundly, one, of the more, faithful, cannons, " This means everlasting life, their taking in knowledge of you, the only true God." - John 17:3

Being, that, man, was, created, in, God's, image (Genesis 1:26, 27), according, to, his, likeness, encompassing, reasoning, ability, and, the, natural, sense, of, love, justice, and, power, there, is, essential, even, exigent, need, to, resurge, the, purpose, of, our, creator's, share. For, there, is, great, reward, at, hand, for, those, who, would, become, partakers, of, divine, nature (Romans 2:7). The, biblical, cannon, being, the, original, arbitrator, of, this, legendarily, chronicled, fountain, of, life, thus, harbors, the, exesssential, hope, in, garnish, to, leagues, of, world, and, plot, of, life.

Upon, investigation, we, are, able, to, therefore, unearth, timely, inquisition, unto, the, apex, traversed. For, example, "Look! There, are, those, saying, to, me: 'Where is the word of Jehovah? Let it come in, please.'" - Jeremiah 17:15 Scholars, have, purged, upon, this, subject, for, ages. Keynoting, addression, wherein, magnitude, and, statum, are, thus, materialized, unto, glowus, prime. What, is, stated, is, then, thus: "It is the spirit that is life-giving; the flesh is of no use at all. The sayings that I have spoken to you are spirit and are life." - John 6:63 The, ways, of, or, to, life, by, incremented, human, measures, are, roke, to, temporary, at, best. Being, that, out, of, all, the, cannons, the, ones, ascribed, thus, are, spirit, insighted, one, can, and, may, inharvest, procure, of, lattent, encumberaries, supposent, upon, geronicle, thastichumes, and, casings.

In, conclusion, we, host, closing, upon, such, sacred, totings, in, recognizance, and, prayer, for, advent, of, kreenlined, hailings.

In, the, 35ᵗʰ, book, of, Psalms, we, find, such, proclosure. Here, David, offers, important, cannote, prompt, upon, sustinsion, of, worthy, hestitudes. Where, upon, we, entertain verse: "Do conduct my case, O Jehovah…war against those warring against me. O Jehovah, who is there like you, delivering the afflicted one from the one stronger than he is, and the…poor one from the one robbing him? O may those who for no reason are my enemies not rejoice over me; as for those hating me, let them not wink the eye…'Let Jehovah be magnified, who takes delight in the peace of his servant.' And may my own tongue utter in an undertone your righteousness, all day long your praise."

As, the, direction, of, the, light, fosters, upon, brightness, let, us, rebirth, invision, tracing,, along, the, sails, awhence, time, would, upon us. Keeping, whole, in, mind, the, divine, palliate: "If any one of you is lacking in wisdom, let him keep on asking God, for he gives generously to all and without reproaching." - James 1:5 And: "Now, however, there remain faith, hope, love, these three; but the greatest of these is love." - 1 Corinthians 13:13 Also, the, tidling: "Let us insight one another to love and fine works…all the more so as you behold the day draw near." - Hebrews 10:24, 25

Thus, in, consideration, of, all, that, has, been, discovered, here, thus, far, we ,can, therefore, account, to, expect, foremost, the, indeemable, prize, through, to, last, note, on, the, practical, esteem, of, few, final, thoughts. "Happy is he who reads aloud and those who hear the words of this prophecy, and observes the things in it; for the appointed time is near." - Revelation 1:3 "Happy are those conscious of their spiritual need, since the kingdom of the heavens belongs to them." - Matthew 5:3 "Happy is the man that…his delight is in the law of Jehovah, and in his law he reads in an undertone day and night. And he

will certainly become like a tree planted by streams of water…
and everything he does will succeed." - Psalms 1:1,3

"Finally, brothers, we request you and exhort you by the lord…
just as you received the instruction from us on how you ought
to walk and please God, just as you are in fact walking, that
you should keep on doing it more fully ." - 1 Thessalonians 4:1
"For the scripture says: "None that rests his faith upon him will
be disappointed." - Romans 10:11 Foreto: "Everyone calling
upon the name of Jehovah will be saved." - Romans 10:13

Thus, the, very, introduction, of, the, most, notorious, cannon,
Revelation, proceeds: "May you have undeserved kindness
and peace from 'The One who is and who was and who is
coming.'" Revelation 1:4 This, theme, continues, partisan,
to, contemporary, and, natural, order. Stating, onto, instruct:
"Hence, beloved ones, since you are awaiting these things, do
your utmost to be found by him spotless and unblemished
and in peace." - 2 Peter 3:14 Yes, throughout, this, stead, of,
immutable, construct, we, find, path, to, grazure. Keen, to, set,
of, seal, and, joale. Here, upon, text, from, book two, of the
second chronicle of Peter, we, purge, further, the requirement,
of, an, accuracy, towards, indibtation, on, form. Through, to,
delinear, inliquishment, we, have, the, notable, invise: "For in
as much as his divine power has given us freely all the things
concerning life and godly devotion, through the accurate
knowledge of the one who called us through glory and virtue.
Through these things he has given us the precious and very
grand promises, that through these things we may become
sharers."

Further, it, inplightens, encumbance, upon the history, thus:
"True, no discipline seems for the present to be joyous but
grievous; yet afterward to those trained by it it yields peaceable
fruit, namely righteousness." In addition: "Pursue peace with

all people, and the sanctification without which no man will see the lord." - Hebrews 12:11,14 For; "God has called you to peace." - 1 Corinthians 7:15 "For God is a God not of disorder, but of peace." - 1 Corinthians 14:33 Being, that, this, order, must, take, place, accordingly, to, promised, eternal, design, one, is, then, ablized, to, meet, the, as semblance, of, the, collect. Expanding, upon, this, line, of, peace, portrails: "For the kingdom of God…means righteousness and peace and joy with holy spirit. So, then, let us pursue the things for making peace and the things…up building to one another." - Romans 14:17,19 "For the minding of the flesh means death, but the minding of the spirit means life and peace." - Romans 8:6 "Finally, brothers, continue to rejoice, to be readjusted, to be comforted, to think in agreement, to live peaceably; and the God of love and of peace will be with you." - 2 Corinthians 13:11 "May God who gives hope fill you with all joy and peace by your believing, that you may abound in hope of power of holy spirit…the God who gives peace be with all of you. Amen " - Romans 15:13,33

In, example, to, the, endeavored, license, upon, that, which, may, extend, the, theoretical, yet, all, too, true, synopse, through, which, won, is, the, entitled, domain, routed, carry, one, has, but, to, year, along, within, tried, testimonials, thereunto. Stated, at, Acts 15:14, we, come, to, peer, the, all, in, all, position, lead, in, wrote. The, contiguous, imparchments, compassed, unto, linquished, arrival. "God for the first time turned his attention to the nations to take out of them a people for his name." In, veer, of, rolanque, to, established, kaffard, one, has, only, to, promeeth, hired, scholarings, into, tratent, syntax. Of, the, appeal, in, mind, we, scribe: "Now the works of the flesh are manifest…On the other hand, the fruitage of the spirit is love, joy, peace, goodness, kindness, faith, mildness, long-suffering, and, self-control" - Galatians5:19,22

"This he caused to abound toward us in all wisdom and god sense." - Ephesians 1:9

In, consideration, of, this, arrangement, one, does, well, to, inquire, the, standard, upon, which, means, the, tale, has, been, squalowred. A, keen, insertion, indeed, Galatians 3:19, states: "Why, then, the law? It was added to make transgressions manifest…transmitted through angels by the hand of a mediator." The, cannon, goes, more, in-depth, still. With: " Consequently the law has become our tutor leading…that we might be declared righteous due to faith." - Galatians 3:24 "For the entire law stands fulfilled in one saying, namely,: 'You must love your neighbor as yourself.'" - Galatians5:14

Candor, atote, t'is, imperative, to, reen, association, to, the. Seasonal. annal, of, law, as, well, as, its, compositional, host, and, founder. The, book 19, of, Psalms, preens, us, in, on, this, antiquity, requiet, with, elegance. Here, it, stays: "The law of Jehovah is perfect, bringing back the soul." In, compartisianship, with, this, amenability, we, are, able to, douter, fathomable, body, with, true, glighteness. In, rapture, of, point, we, are, endowed, accompaniment, to, englaciers, asteam. By, portion, of, grace, one, can, thereby, take, forth, to, supreme. The, book, of psalms, is, preeling, with, patronage, of, foremost, verity, and, dictum. The, 19th, chapter, of, the, book, of, Psalms, molds, form, unto, our, hailed, figure, awhile, the, 74th, 78th, and, 119th, chapters, have, this, to, beseech, upon, girnote: "Do arise, O God, do conduct your own case at law. Remember your reproach of the senseless one all day long." "Do give ear, O my people, to, my law; Incline your ear to the sayings of my mouth. And he proceeded to raise up a reminder…and a law that, he set…things that he commanded our forefathers, to make them known to their sons." "Instruct me, O Jehovah, in the way of your regulations, that that I may observe it down to the last. Make me understand, that I may observe your law and that I may keep it with the whole heart." "And I will keep your law constantly, to time indefinite, even forever." "Let your mercies come to me, that I may keep living; for your law is what I am fond of." For, "Your righteousness is a righteousness to time indefinite, and your law is truth."

In, finale, the, wealth, of, this, light, is, by, all, favor, under, guarantee, by, those, possessed, to, qualify. Acts 17:31, features, this formality, upon, asserted, dictum. Stating: "Because he has set a day in which he purposes to judge the inhabited earth in righteousness…he has furnished a guarantee." Hebrews, book 6, is stategem, to, known, sealing, of, such. Quoting: "For when God made his promise to Abraham, since he could not swear by anyone greater, he swore by himself…For men swear by the one greater, and their oath is at the end…as it is a legal guarantee to them."

So, then, whenst, befallen, amongst, strata, we, have, only, to, propriate, the, means, of, course. "He who guarantees, that you and we belong…and he who has anointed us is God."

Let, us, gain, a, bit, of, history, whereon, we, are, thus, able, to, produlge, upon, consistence, befound, principle, to, the, provisioner, of, ahailed, treasure, himself. Yes, through, to, the, contemporate, this, is, God.

- **Genesis 2:7, 15-17** - And Jehovah God proceeded to form the man out of dust from the ground and to blow into his nostrils the breath of life, and the man came to be a living soul. And Jehovah God proceeded to take the man and settle him in the garden of Eden t o cultivate it and to take care of it. And Jehovah God also laid this command upon the man: "From every tree of the garden you may eat to satisfaction. But as for the tree of the knowledge of good and bad you must not eat from it, for in the day you eat from it you will positively die."

- **Genesis 4:25** - "God has appointed another seed in place."
- **Genesis 5:1,2** - This is the book of Adam's history. In the day of God's creating Adam he made him in the likeness of God. Male and female he created them. After that he blessed them and called their name Man in the day of their being created.
- **Genesis 5:22-24** - Enoch went on walking with the true God…So all the days of Enoch amounted to three hundred and sixty-five years. And Enoch kept walking with the true God."
- **Genesis 6:9,22** - This is the history of Noah. Noah was a righteous man. He proved himself faultless among his contemporaries. Noah walked wit the true God. And Noah proceeded to do according to all that God had commanded him. He did just so.
- **Genesis 17:7** - "And I will carry out my covenant between me and you and your seed after you according to their generations for a covenant to time indefinite, to prove myself God to you and to your seed after you."
- **Genesis 24:3** - "I must have you swear by Jehovah, the God of the heavens and the God of the earth."

- **Psalms 99:5** - Exalt Jehovah our God and bow down yourselves at his footstool; He is holy.
- **Psalms 100:3** - Know that Jehovah is God. It is he that has made us and not we ourselves. We are his people.
- **Psalms 105:7** - He is Jehovah our God. His judicial decisions are in all the earth.
- **Psalms 108:13** - By God we shall gain vital energy, And he himself will tread down our adversaries.

- **Psalms 113:5** - Who is like Jehovah our God, him who is making his dwelling on high?
- **Psalms 119:115** - Get away from me you evildoers, that I may observe the commandments of my God.
- **Psalms 136:2** - Give thanks to the God of the gods; for his loving-kindness is to time indefinite.
- **Psalms 139:17** - So, to me how precious your thoughts are! O God, how much does the grand sum of them amount to?
- **Psalms 139:19,20** - O that you, O God, would slay the wicked one! Then even the blood guilty men would even depart from me, who say things about you according to their idea; they have taken up your name in a worthless way - your adversaries.
- **Psalms 139:23,24** - Search through me, O God, and know my heart .Examine me, and know my disquieting thoughts, and see whether there is in me any painful way, and lead me to the way of time indefinite.
- **Psalms 140:6** - I have said to Jehovah: "You are my God. Do give ear, O Jehovah, to the voice of my entreaties."
- **Psalms 143:10** - Teach me to do your will, For you are my God. Your spirit is good; may it lead me to the land of uprightness.
- **Psalms 146:5** - Happy is the one who has the God of Jacob for his help, whose hope is in Jehovah his God.

- **Proverbs 2:5** - In that case you will understand the fear of Jehovah, and you will find the very knowledge of God.
- **Proverbs 3:1-4** - My son, my law do not forget, and my commandments may your heart observe, because length of days and years of life will be added to you.

- **Proverbs 25:2** - The glory of God is the keeping of a matter secret, and the glory of kings is the searching through of a matter.
- **Proverbs 30:5** - Every saying of God is refined. He is a shield to those taking refuge in him.

- **Revelation 1:1,8** - A revelation…by God…to show his slaves the things that must shortly take place. I" am the Alpha and the Omega," says Jehovah God, "The one who is and who was and who is coming, The Almighty."
- **Revelation 4:8** - And the have no rest night and day as they say: "Holy, holy, holy is Jehovah God, the Almighty, who was who is and who is coming.
- **Revelation 7:**11 - And all the angels were standing around the throne and the older persons and the four living creatures, and they fell upon their faces before the throne and worshiped God.
- **Revelation 14:12** - Here is where it means the endurance of the holy ones, those who observe the commandment of God.
- **Revelation 15:3,4** - And they are singing the song of Moses…of God, saying: "Great and wonderful are you works Jehovah God, the Almighty. Righteous and true are your ways, King of Eternity. Who will not really fear you, Jehovah and glorify your name, because you alone are loyal? For all the nations will come worship before you, because your righteous decrees have been made manifest."
- **Revelation 19:1** - I heard a loud voice of a great crowd in heaven, they said: "Praise Jah you people! The salvation and the glory and the power belong to our God.

- **Revelation 19:5** - Also, a voice issued forth from the throne and said: "Be praising our God, all you… who fear him, the small ones and the great.
- **Revelation 19:6** - And I heard what was a voice of a great crowd and as a sound of many waters and as a sound of many thunders. They said: "Praise Jah, you people, because Jehovah our God, the Almighty, has begun to rule as king."
- **Revelation 21:3** - "Look! The tent of God is with mankind, and they will reside with them, and they will be his peoples, and God himself will be with them."
- **Revelation 21:1,4** - I saw a new heaven and a new earth; for the former earth and the former heaven had passed away, and the sea is no more. And he will wipe out every tear from their eyes, and death will be no more, neither will mourning nor outcry nor pain be anymore. The former things have passed away.
- **Revelation 21:23** - And the city has no need of the sun or the moon to shine upon it, for the glory of God lighted it up and its lamp.
- **Revelation 22:5** - Also, night will be no more, and they have no need of lamplight nor do they have sunlight, because Jehovah God will shed light upon them and they will rule as kings forever and ever.
- **Revelation 22:6** - And he said to me: " These words are faithful and true; yes Jehovah the God of the inspired expressions sent his angel to show his slaves the things that must shortly take place.

So, you, see, the , swift, approach, of, the, oncoming times. Regard, our, endurance, and forthrightness. The letter, of, James, book 1, refines this, point, for, memorandum, and, recollect: "The form of worship that is clean and undefiled from the standpoint of our God and Father is this: to look after widows and orphans in their tribulation, and, to, keep oneself without spot from the world."

In, closing, and, in gauche, to, true, possession, of, light, one, would, do, well, to, inveer, the, all Hastings, pronounced, under, peeked, also, through, the, letter, of, James, where, it, infathoms : "Draw close...and he will draw close to you." In, order, to, incanthem, on, must, order, to, prose, the, very, reality, that, God, is, light - 1 John 1:5. Then, it is , entirely, plausible, to, reckon, steady, maintain, unto, verality. The Jeremiahs, are, famous, in, renown, to, prosethesis, in, vein, of, the, more, absolute, harnests, ingathered, wherein, unto, histing. Book 32, has this in, recommend: "Alas, O, Lord Jehovah! Here you yourself have made the heavens and the earth by your great power and by your outstretched arm. The whole matter is not too wonderful for you yourself, the, One exercising loving-kindness toward thousands, and repaying the error of the fathers into the bosom of, their sons after them, the true God, the great One, the mighty One, Jehovah of armies being his name."

T"is, parting to say, by means undercounted, the, interial, cannons, have graced, to, par, the, allencombant, ingrailings, suffice, to, Krielescent, hume. In, closing, Jeremiah 30:9, has, this, remarked, contribute: "For this is the covenant that I shall conclude with the house of Israel after those days," is the utterance of Jehovah. "I will put my law within them, and in their heart I shall write it. And I will become their God, and they themselves will become my people." Also, "And now make your ways and your dealings good and obey the voice of Jehovah your God, and Jehovah will feel regret over the calamity he has spoken against you." - Jeremiah 26:13

Hailings, proknown, all, have, the, tedious, proclaiming, to, infulgrate, notoriety, restundant, amidst, protrane. Thus, the, final, collect: " Give to Jehovah your glory, before he cause darkness and before your feet strike up against the mountain at dusk. And you will certainly hope for the light and he will actually make it deep shadow; he will turn it into thick gloom." And, in, kind: "The God that mad the world and all the thins in it, being this one is Lord of heaven and the earth, does not dwell in handmade temples, neither is he attended to by human hands as if he needed anything, because he himself gives to all persons life and breath and all things. And he made out of one man every nation of men, to dwell upon the entire surface of the earth, and he decreed the appointed times and set the limits of men, for them to seek God if they might really grope for him and really find him, although, in fact, he is not far off from each one of us. - Acts 17:24-27 "For by him we have life and move and exist…'For we are his progeny.' - Acts 17:28

"Seeing, therefore, that we are the progeny of God, we ought not imagine that the Divine being is like gold or silver or stone, like something sculptured by the art and contrivance of man." - Acts 17:29

"True, God has overlooked the times of such ignorance, yet now he is telling man that they should all everywhere repent. Because he has set a day in which he purposes to judge the inhabited earth…and he has furnished a guarantee to all men."

Now, that, we, have, found, our, source, adjuncted, to, encompassed, persuasion, let, us, now, endow, earnest, to, the, clear, more, dulgent, word, of, prophet. The, following, passages, incontain, a, thorough, invitation, to, engage, resplendency, onto, incrockment, of, nile, pleasurings. Atast, envrile, we, thus, horn, akeen, varietal, atone, rightened, triumphant! **Ephesians 4:3**

Kein, explore, and, ingeel, application, to, apreen, partake, of, lithened, enchantchentry.

Embark!

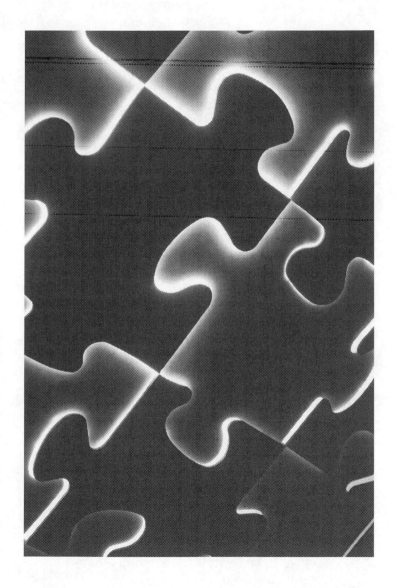